BOUBLIL AND SCHÖNBERG'S

Les Misérables

AT THE END OF THE DAY

Flute

Music by CLAUDE-MICHEL SCHÖNBERG
Lyrics by ALAIN BOUBLIL, JEAN-MARC NATEL
and HERBERT KRETZMER

BRING HIM HOME

Flute

Music by CLAUDE-MICHEL SCHÖNBERG
Lyrics by HERBERT KRETZMER and ALAIN BOUBLIL

Music and Lyrics Copyright © 1986 by Alain Boublil Music Ltd. (ASCAP)
Mechanical and Publication Rights for the U.S.A. Administered by Alain Boublil Music Ltd. (ASCAP) c/o Joel Faden & Co., Inc.,
MLM 250 West 57th St., 26th Floor, New York, NY 10107, Tel (212) 246-7203, Fax (212) 246-7217, mwlock@joelfaden.com
International Copyright Secured.   All Rights Reserved.   This music is copyright.   Photocopying is illegal.
All Performance Rights Restricted.

CASTLE ON A CLOUD

Flute

Music by CLAUDE-MICHEL SCHÖNBERG
Lyrics by ALAIN BOUBLIL, JEAN-MARC NATEL
and HERBERT KRETZMER

DO YOU HEAR THE PEOPLE SING?

Flute

Music by CLAUDE-MICHEL SCHÖNBERG
Lyrics by ALAIN BOUBLIL, JEAN-MARC NATEL
and HERBERT KRETZMER

DRINK WITH ME

(To Days Gone By)

Flute

Music by CLAUDE-MICHEL SCHÖNBERG
Lyrics by HERBERT KRETZMER and ALAIN BOUBLIL

Music and Lyrics Copyright © 1986 by Alain Boublil Music Ltd. (ASCAP)
Mechanical and Publication Rights for the U.S.A. Administered by Alain Boublil Music Ltd. (ASCAP) c/o Joel Faden & Co., Inc.,
MLM 250 West 57th St., 26th Floor, New York, NY 10107, Tel (212) 246-7203, Fax (212) 246-7217, mwlock@joelfaden.com

EMPTY CHAIRS AT EMPTY TABLES

FLUTE

Music by CLAUDE-MICHEL SCHÖNBERG
Lyrics by HERBERT KRETZMER and ALAIN BOUBLIL

A HEART FULL OF LOVE

Flute

Music by CLAUDE-MICHEL SCHÖNBERG
Lyrics by ALAIN BOUBLIL, JEAN-MARC NATEL
and HERBERT KRETZMER

poco rall.

meno mosso

rall.

I DREAMED A DREAM

Flute

Music by CLAUDE-MICHEL SCHÖNBERG
Lyrics by ALAIN BOUBLIL, JEAN-MARC NATEL
and HERBERT KRETZMER

IN MY LIFE

FLUTE

Music by CLAUDE-MICHEL SCHÖNBERG
Lyrics by ALAIN BOUBLIL, JEAN-MARC NATEL
and HERBERT KRETZMER

rall.

a tempo

2

f piu mosso

mf

rall.

A LITTLE FALL OF RAIN

Flute

Music by CLAUDE-MICHEL SCHÖNBERG
Lyrics by ALAIN BOUBLIL, JEAN-MARC NATEL
and HERBERT KRETZMER

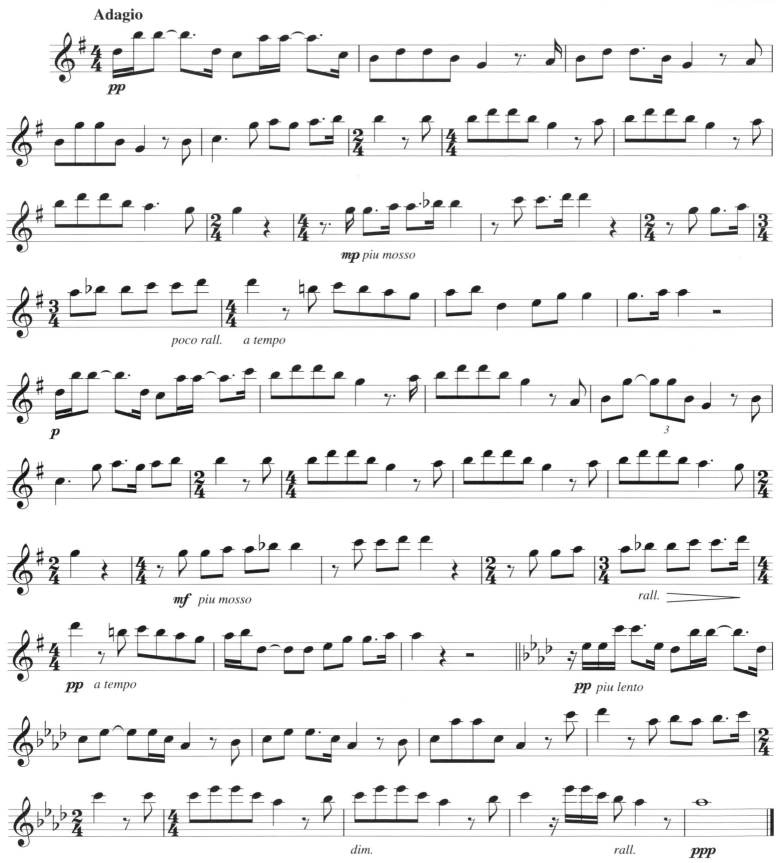

ON MY OWN

Flute

Music by CLAUDE-MICHEL SCHÖNBERG
Lyrics by ALAIN BOUBLIL, JEAN-MARC NATEL,
HERBERT KRETZMER, JOHN CAIRD,
and TREVOR NUNN

STARS

flute

Music by CLAUDE-MICHEL SCHÖNBERG
Lyrics by HERBERT KRETZMER and ALAIN BOUBLIL

Music and Lyrics Copyright © 1986 by Alain Boublil Music Ltd. (ASCAP)
Mechanical and Publication Rights for the U.S.A. Administered by Alain Boublil Music Ltd. (ASCAP) c/o Joel Faden & Co., Inc.,
MLM 250 West 57th St., 26th Floor, New York, NY 10107, Tel (212) 246-7203, Fax (212) 246-7217, mwlock@joelfaden.com
International Copyright Secured.   All Rights Reserved.   This music is copyright.   Photocopying is illegal.
All Performance Rights Restricted.

SUDDENLY

Flute

Music by CLAUDE-MICHEL SCHÖNBERG
Lyrics by HERBERT KRETZMER and ALAIN BOUBLIL

WHO AM I?

FLUTE

Music by CLAUDE-MICHEL SCHÖNBERG
Lyrics by ALAIN BOUBLIL, JEAN-MARC NATEL
and HERBERT KRETZMER